Walking Around in South Stre...

Discoveries in ...
Old Shipping ...

Ellen Fletcher Rosebrock

South Street Seaport Museum
16 Fulton Street, New York

The most genuine appreciation is expressed by the author to
those whose efforts on its behalf made this book possible.

Alan Burnham
David Canright
Norma Stanford
Terry Walton
The New York City Landmarks
    Preservation Commission,
    Research Division

Publication made possible by a grant from the New York
State Council on the Arts.

Distributed by Interbook Inc., 545 Eighth Ave., New York, N.Y. 10018

PREFACE

Echoing to sailors' songs and draymen's curses, old brick streaked by many rains and windows dazzled by rising suns across the tides of the East River, the old buildings of the South Street waterfront have survived to our day. They house lively memories and meanings. They survive from a time when words and deeds were bolder in New York—when people talked with a salt savor to their words, a wholeness and bite in discourse as one can catch in old papers of the time; and they walked with a proprietary swagger, a sense of owning and belonging that you catch, in old photographs, in the stance of the hostler and the merchant prince alike. Mutual respect in a class-conscious society? Or merely a kind of settled dependence, which one can see symbolized in the old buildings of South Street, leaning against each other ("out of plumb" as our architectural historian puts it in the opening sentence of this admirable guide) for mutual support?

Who knows? The fact is that the historic neighborhood survives to be enjoyed today. The story of people's work before our time also survives, and is celebrated here. We recall Captain Joseph Rose, who built his house and shop on Water Street three years before the Revolution when we see that house standing today, the third oldest building on Manhattan Island. We know General Ebenezer Stevens who won glory in the War for Independence by his countinghouses on Front and South Streets where he based his traffic in exotic liquors from 1798. There are others, too, whose lives touched here once, adding little by little to that composite character that the newest visitor can feel walking into our South Street neighborhood, once famous 'round the world as the "street of ships."

South Street is a monumental collection of ships and buildings weathering some kind of passage through the seas of time. It is a most visible argument in favor of things being (in an overcalculating and sometimes, today, despairing society), a little more natural, a little more mutually dependent, a little out of plumb.

Hurrah for old humanity! Let us honor its cause here in South Street, where its labors are so clearly, vividly, memorably expressed in the shapes of the housing and sea chariots of an earlier day. Let us find new meanings in these old roots, so we can get on with the work of the City today with a little more grace, a little more dignity, a new sense of joy in the work. The South Street Museum plans to reclaim for the purpose some of these ancient, leaning structures—to stabilize them, not to rebuild them, but definitely to care for them.

And if you care to be part of these efforts, join the Museum! You'll find in the words of the old story, "a hearty welcome waiting." Your help is needed, because our buildings, our ships, our story have no meaning and no future without you.

Peter Stanford
President,
South Street Seaport Museum

INTRODUCTION

Mossy, grayed, often out of plumb, the ancient buildings in the Fulton Market neighborhood have a strong character that the passage of time has left them, dropping successive veils of heavy use, change, grime and neglect over their once-crisp brick fronts. The character is there—anyone can sense it, but to understand it specifically, to know the substance behind the illusion you must look back far into the history of the neighborhood's experience.

The seven-block enclave of warehouses and stores has not always been so distinct from the rest of the city, but once directly reflected the rise and progress of the downtown business community, sharing its booms and depressions and echoing them in the fortunes of its occupants and its buildings.

The South Street-Front Street-Water Street strip on the East River is all "made" land, created from the tidelands by successive periods of landfill and wharf building between 1686 and 1820. The strip was, during its 19th century history, literally the gateway to the City, wrapping the grander inner portions: Wall Street with its handsome Georgian and Greek Revival buildings, the financial palaces of an earlier day; Broadway with its brilliant retail shops (extravagantly lit with gas from an early date, and kept open late into the night); and, closer to the East River shipping center, the wholesale shops of Pearl Street, "the richest street in the City."

Little remains of the evanescent inner New York of the 19th century—an occasional high-style landmark well cared for, and scattered single and grouped buildings which to varying degrees retain evidence of an early origin. Continued prosperity and the New York characteristic of pursuing progress have replaced most of the buildings in downtown New York several times over.

The dedicated searcher in downtown New York, though, will find his rambles through Whitehall Street, State Street, Pearl Street, Stone Street, Hanover Square and Wall Street, Front Street and Water Street well rewarded when he finds the single and clustered buildings that were houses, saloons, stores, shipping offices, mercantile exchanges and banks a century or more ago. Three excellent guides direct walkers through the narrow old streets and byways: Norval White's and Elliot Willensky's *AIA Guide to New York City*, beautifully illustrated and arranged by district; Ada Louise Huxtable's *Classic New York*, organized by architectural type with photographs illustrating characteristics of buildings of different styles and types—equipping the aspiring architectural sleuth to make his own discoveries and class them by period; and Catrina Ten Eyck Seymour's small map and guide to the downtown area, available at the New-York Historical Society, which is easiest to use and includes her own drawings of several important buildings.

It is after you've pursued the elusive, often hidden old building through the narrow downtown streets that the miracle of the seven-block survival here on the East River commercial strip assumes its real significance. Here the sun shines at mid-day into the narrowest streets, the sky somehow seems closer overhead than in the downtown canyons. Here we can see how the City was supposed to look when street widths were determined in the 18th and early 19th centuries.

To prepare for your walk, think of the early, hurried days when these streets were laid out, when the land-hungry city men pushed their shores street by street out into land claimed from their harbor. If these buildings seem a bit cracked and leaning, it's because the merchants who built them were in such a hurry to get going that they couldn't wait for their artificial land to finish settling before they framed up their stores and countinghouses and sank their stone foundations into the shifty mud of the landfill.

To get to the beginning of all this, think back for a moment further than these streets themselves, to the first European involvement with Manhattan Island. Early in the 17th century, even before there were houses here, or a fort, there was the harbor itself and there was trade. At the time of the burning of the *Tiger* in 1614 we know that at least a dozen Dutch ships were using the harbor on trading missions with the Indians. Only the rudest of shelters welcomed the Dutchmen on Manhattan's shores, but their commercial visits here were many. It is true indeed that "New York was a seaport before it was a City."

During the 17th century the little outpost grew from a lonely colony in the woods to a respectable commercial town. In 1672 New York became an English colony, steadily growing on its trade, stimulated by the wars with the French over Canada. Early growth was quiet, and its process was interrupted by the American Revolution.

It was after 1783 (the evacuation of the British troops from New York) that the City began to express itself in a startling way. Not a month after the evacuation merchants were sending out ships on ambitious globe-spanning junkets. The remote commercial outpost was suddenly America's major city. By 1790 it exceeded the other contenders in population, and by 1800 the tonnage of its port was greater than that of either Boston or Philadelphia.

New York had just begun to climb in 1800. From then until the beginning of the Civil War, the City, firmly rooted in its mercantile tradition, was what its harbor had made it—and its harbor was ruled by South Street. There the ruling class of New York, the merchants, had their tall, proud countinghouses from whose small-paned windows they surveyed the channel waters and the ships lying at anchor along the wharves. Running back from South Street the slips and lanes lined with smaller houses led to Front and Water streets, where the tradesmen and the warehouses (to say nothing of the saloons and boarding houses) completed the waterfront community.

Following the War of 1812 South Street and New York knew unprecedented prosperity. In January of 1818 the Black Ball Line of Liverpool packets (the first regular transatlantic freight and passenger line) began sailing from South Street just south of Peck Slip, near our present Pier 17. "From the sailing of this packet," wrote seedsman Grant Thorburn in his memoirs, "we may date the day whence the commerce of New York began to increase seven-fold." In 1825 the opening of the Erie Canal channeled farm and industrial produce from the Middle West through New York harbor and out in the City's ships for export. Five hundred new mercantile firms were founded in New York during that year alone, but as Robert G. Albion reminds us in his classic *Rise of New York Port,* it was South Street—the seaport—that created the canal, that generated the money and the business to build it, not the canal that created South Street.

During the second half of the 1820s nearly all descriptions of the City recorded the nearly unnavigable state of the sidewalks due to mud and the impedimenta of successful commerce. Crates, barrels, boxes and carts burst from every overloaded store to pile on the street. The 1840s and 1850s saw the high noon of New

York's maritime empire. The China trade, led by A. A. Low & Brothers, infused the streets with exotic glamor. Japan was opened in 1854, and clippers from this port were carrying thousands of settlers to California. The South Street countinghouses, formerly occupied by one or two firms, began to crowd up; sail makers, riggers, figurehead carvers and other waterfront businesses joined the merchants in their buildings.

From the 1860s on, the neighborhood declined in importance. The new giant steamships went to new deepwater piers on the North River (Hudson). The commercial center—except for the insurance industry around John Street, the investment community centering on Wall Street, the great shipping firms near the island tip, clustering round Whitehall Street and lower Broadway—crept toward midtown. A kind of raffishness replaced early commercial opulence, and as the sailing ships departed, one by one, on their last voyages, leaving behind in the towers of Lower Manhattan a world-renowned monument to the business they'd brought here, a kind of parochial somnolence began to replace the bustle and world-wide outlook of an earlier age.

Today the South Street neighborhood stirs to new, intensely local but also cosmopolitan vitality as the South Street Museum brings together visitors, ships, discourse, educational programs and the reviving bustle of shops and eateries which will make the area again a market of goods, of ideas—and of people.

MAP 1   5

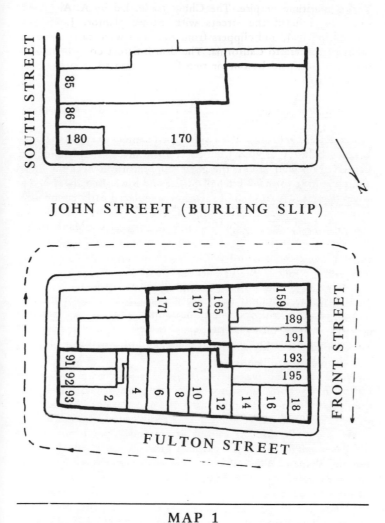

SOUTH STREET

85

86

180   170

JOHN STREET (BURLING SLIP)

171   167   165   159
189
191
193
195

91   92   93   2   4   6   8   10   12   14   16   18

FRONT STREET

FULTON STREET

N

MAP 1

Begin the walk on Fulton Street near the corner of Front.

Fulton is the only downtown street which runs uninterrupted from the Hudson to the East River, its numbering continuous from east to west. This grandness, though, dates only to 1814

*Fulton Ferry Terminal, built of cast iron for the
Union Ferry Company in 1863.* D. T. Valentine's Manual, 1864.

when a new street was ordered opened to connect Beekman's Slip
(the present Fulton Street between Pearl Street and the River)
and Fair Street (the portion extending east of Broadway to Cliff
Street). In September of 1816 the whole thoroughfare was united
under the name of Fulton, to honor Robert Fulton, who had died
in 1815. Fulton was the developer of the steam ferryboat and
owner of the Brooklyn ferry which began here in 1814, running
to Fulton Street in Brooklyn.

While the ferry was active, Fulton Street terminated at the
Fulton Ferry house, first a wooden structure of classical design,
then a handsome cast iron building of 1863, designed by architect
John Kellum and made by Badger's Architectural Iron Works.

As you walk through Fulton Street today you'll notice that
the pavement consists of brownish gray stones, each about the
size and shape of a loaf of bread. These stones were known as the
"Russ Pavement" or "Belgian block" (as the paving type was
claimed to be a Belgian invention). New England quarries supplied much of this stone. Fulton was one of the first New York
streets to have its cobblestones replaced by the blocks in 1854.

★SCHERMERHORN ROW
**2-18 Fulton Street; 91, 92, 93 South Street; 195 & 197 Front
Street**

Stand on the corner of Fulton and Front Streets, looking at
the Georgian commercial block known as Schermerhorn Row. It

MAP 1   7

Fulton Street looking east toward the ferry terminal, circa 1825.
Schermerhorn Row, looking as it did when first built, stands at the right.
Barrels line the flagged sidewalks, and a pig with her shoats
dashes gaily down Fulton Street in celebration of Spring.

was in 1726 that the Schermerhorn family began to buy land in this neighborhood.

Arnout Schermerhorn of the third generation of American Schermerhorns, a shipmaster, purchased land east of Pearl (then Queen) Street from his father-in-law Johannes Beekman in three successive increments on April 21, 1726; February 10, 1729 and April 3, 1729. The land was part of a larger grant that had been made to Beekman by the City in 1719.

Two generations later Peter Schermerhorn the elder (1749-1826) became the member of his family most active in this neighborhood. He was called "Captain" Schermerhorn, and was a shipowner as well as a merchant. His ships were in the coastal trade between New York and Charleston.

During the British occupation of New York in the Revolution, Schermerhorn, a patriot, moved upstate near Poughkeepsie, where his vessels could be kept safe from seizure, and where his son Peter Jr. was born in 1781. After his return to New York, he established himself as a ship chandler on Water Street near "the Crane Wharf" (now Beekman Street).

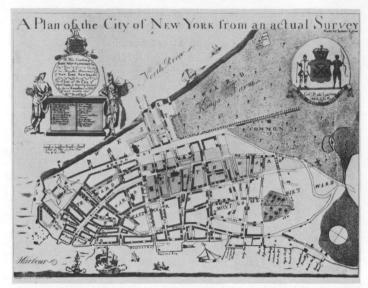

James Lyne's Survey of New York, made in 1728.

On the 2nd of December, 1793, Peter Schermerhorn consolidated the family water lot holdings (still unfilled) on the south side of Beekman Slip (presently Fulton Street) east of Front Street, and bought the entire parcel himself. A New York water lot lay between the marks of high tide and low tide, and was therefore under water half the time. To make it usable, its owner had to build it up with landfill, constructing wooden "cribs" into which he would dump enough cartloads of refuse to fill it up to street level. A display in the 16 Fulton Street Museum illustrates the type of refuse one finds in this fill: old porcelain, pottery, glassware—broken, cast-off things. The Taylor-Roberts Plan of 1797 shows his land partially filled, and the Bridges map, surveyed in 1807, shows the entire holding complete, with an alley separating it from George Codwise's land on the south side of the block.

Beekman Slip had not yet been filled, although the Bridges Map, published in 1811, which perhaps shows a projected condition, showed the fill complete. In December of 1813, however, it was selected as the Manhattan terminus of Robert Fulton's Brooklyn ferry because it actually was filled.

MAP 1   9

In 1811, Schermerhorn began to build his block-long row. Beginning on the water side, Nos. 91, 92 & 93 South Street, and Nos. 2, 4, 6, 8, 10 & 12 Fulton Street were built that year, with the remainder, Nos. 14, 16 & 18 Fulton Street together with 195 & 197 Front Street following in 1812.

Even though these tall, handsome stores seem more conveniently located and more spacious than the building the Schermerhorn chandlery occupied at 243 Water Street, the new row must have been intended as an income producer, as the family firm never occupied it—all stores were leased to other merchants. In 1812, and in 1815 through 1817, though, John Peter Schermer-

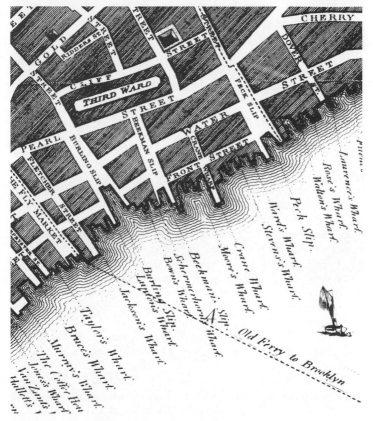

The Taylor-Roberts Plan of New York (detail), *1797.*
(The New York Public Library.)

horn, a son of Peter the elder who had not joined the old firm, ran his own ship chandlery first in the 12 Fulton Street store, then in No. 14.

Peter Schermerhorn had chosen well when he selected the site for his row. In 1793 when he bought his land the markets were north at Peck Slip and south at Maiden Lane, and the area here was only a place between the more important wharfs and slips.

The Bridges Survey of New York (detail), *made in 1807.*
(The New York Public Library.)

MAP 1   11

Hardly had he finished building, though, when the Brooklyn Ferry approached him about landing at the foot of his wharf. Because of the ferry, Fulton Street was created and rapidly became one of the busiest in the commercial district. Shortly afterward, the Fulton Market directly across the street became a serious probability, and in 1822 it opened, solidifying Schermerhorn Row's position as one of the most valuable commercial holdings in the City.

The Row was built in the conservative late Georgian-Federal tradition then standard for New York commercial architecture. With its brownstone-quoined arched doors and wide shop windows, wrought-iron second-story balconies, slate-covered roofs and rhythmic chimneys, the Row was strikingly handsome as a block during its first two decades.

Schermerhorn Row was built as a block of warehouses with merchants' counting rooms, not as stores. Its original typical ground-floor design was composed of one arched doorway and one standard-sized double-hung window per building. There were no Georgian or early Federal shop fronts in the Row. By the late 1840s many of the old brick fronts had been replaced by the granite piered shopfronts of the Greek Revival, and ten years after that more were altered with cast-iron columns. All of the Row's ground floors have been several times modified in the ceaseless commercial flux which has been its life.

The upper floors, though, with the exception of two roof changes, a few alterations in window size and the removal of most of the chimneys, remain as built.

Look at the uneven roofline of the Row. The mansard over 2 Fulton Street and 92 and 93 South Street was added in 1868 to increase the capacity of the steamboat hotel (McKinley's, later called the Fulton Ferry Hotel) that occupied it, and the fifth story at No. 12 was an unhappy modification of 1935.

At 2 Fulton Street remains one original arched doorway (with Victorian door), and the adjacent splayed brownstone lintel marks an original ground floor window. This corner store is shown in the William J. Bennet engraving of Fulton Market, published in 1834. Richard S. Williams, the grocery firm shown here in that view, occupied the ground floor store from 1812 until 1863. It was at Williams' that the Long Island mail was collected for distribution by the drivers of local stages.

Nearly all of the earliest tenants in the Row were classified as "merchants." Later occupants had varied trades: grocers, provi-

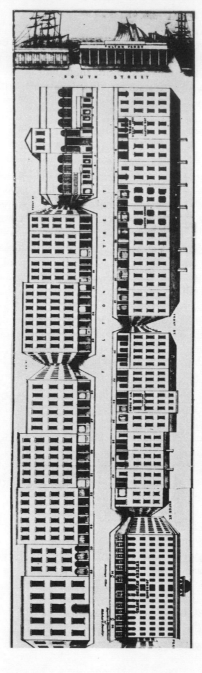

Illuminated Pictorial Directory of Fulton Street, ca. 1848. One of four principal New York streets depicted in illustrated directories, Fulton Street was booming in the late 1840s. Along both sides of the street the granite-piered shopfronts of the Greek Revival outnumber the old Federal-style arched entrances.

MAP 1   13

sioners, eating houses, hotels, liquor shops, taverns, clothiers, clerks, bootmakers, barbers. Even a "factory" later occupied the buildings, tenants making changes to suit their own needs.

At 4 Fulton is Sweet's Restaurant—first located in the Row at No. 8 in 1847. Abraham M. Sweet then called his business a "refectory."

Eagle Bag and Burlap occupied 12 Fulton Street for more than half a century, closing fairly recently. The shop sign advertising "unusual gifts" in neon lights was theirs, and is still in place on the building. An importer of burlap sacking, owner Eli Cohen first supplied the fish market with the cloth they used to cover their "sugar barrels." Later, the inventory was expanded to include exotic curios from faraway ports with which customers of Sweet's and Sloppy Louie's Restaurants were lured into the shop and Cohen's business was increased.

The South Street Seaport Museum's historical displays and development plan may be seen at No. 16.

An astonishing survival from the earliest days of Schermerhorn Row, this arched opening was an original entrance. The Victorian wood doors were installed in the third quarter of the 19th century for the Fulton Ferry Hotel. (Mark Sugg.)

Turn riverward on Fulton Street, then south (right) into South Street.

91 & 92 South Street

92 South Street, still part of Schermerhorn Row, now houses Sloppy Louie's Restaurant, thought by some to make unparalleled bouillabaise; The Sketch Pad, an eating place well known in lower Manhattan, occupies No. 91.

The gas station at the corner of Burling Slip (John Street), built in 1956, replaced three buildings similar to Schermerhorn Row and built in the same year. At this corner was the office of E. K. Collins, founder of the Collins line of transatlantic passenger steamships which once rivalled England's Cunard Line. By 1850, Collins ran four splendid steamships: the *Arctic,* the *Baltic,* the *Atlantic* and the *Pacific.* In 1854 disaster overtook the line. In that year the *Arctic* was sunk in a disgraceful accident off Newfoundland, killing 300 people who might have been saved had the crew behaved more courageously. Collins' own family died in the wreck. Next the *Pacific* simply disappeared, and finally Collins was ruined in the Panic of 1857.

Walk into the wide expanse of John Street, remembering that its unusual width allowed for a wharf on either side of the slip, which was filled in 1835.

★A. A. LOW & BROTHERS
167-171 John Street

The scented mysteries from the Orient, the fabrics, porcelains, spices and teas that filled the holds of the China clippers were the symbols of the great glamorous phase of New York's merchant marine—the China Trade! America's enchantment over its traffic with the Orient was deep and widespread, even as today.

At the very top of the business was the storied firm of A. A. Low & Brothers, founded in 1840 by Abiel Abbot Low, just back from three years in Canton, where he'd learned the China trade from Houqua, legendary Hong patron of young Americans. After the first decade, when the firm was housed with Seth Low (A. A. Low's father, a drug importer) on Fletcher Street, then at 115 South Street, Low built his strikingly handsome granite-faced countinghouse at 167-171 John Street, for which he demolished the old brick structures on the site. The Low firm occupied its building here on Burling Slip from 1850 until after the turn of

MAP 1   15

the century. The cast-iron double storefront was made for the building sometime before 1865.

A great fleet of China clippers was built for the Lows, including *Houqua, Montauk, Samuel Russell, Surprise, Oriental* and *N. B. Palmer,* named for one of the firm's captains. The *Great Republic,* rebuilt after the 1853 fire at Dover Street which cancelled her maiden voyage, also bore the red and yellow house flag of A. A. Low.

After Commodore Perry's expedition in 1854 had opened commerce with Japan, A. A. Low was among the first of the New York merchants who sent ships to the ports of Shimoda, Hakodate and Nagasaki.

The fine old building, set high above a tall basement, has cast-iron piers which once had elaborate Corinthian capitals at the ground floor, and its upper floors have been covered with stucco. When originally built, it was probably as imposing as the granite-faced building across John Street (Nos. 170-176), built ten years earlier and now occupied by the Baker, Carver & Morrell firm of ship chandlers.

170-176 John Street

The Baker, Carver & Morrell ship chandlery has sensitively and intelligently restored the handsome block of granite stores built in 1840 for Hickson W. Field, a commission merchant who bought the three buildings it replaced in 1835.

Except for the stucco-covered A. A. Low & Brothers building facing it across Burling Slip, this is the only all-granite Greek Revival warehouse left in New York's commercial district. Never as common as the type with upper stories of brick, this Boston-originated building form was introduced to New York in 1829 by Ithiel Town with the silk store of Arthur and Lewis Tappan at 122 Pearl Street. The early 19th century commercial ideal is well expressed in this building: the austere gray of its wall pierced by the rhythmic ranges of dark shutterless windows gradually decreasing in size toward the top, and the open colonnade formed by the line of pillars marching across the ground floor facade.

165, 163 & 159 John Street

On the north side of the slip, at 165 John Street, stands the last of the earliest structures built on this blockfront contempora-

neously with Schermerhorn Row on the Fulton Street side. Built
in 1811 for George Codwise, Jr., it was the westernmost in a six-
building row stretching in from South Street and later extended
by Codwise to the corner of Front Street. Number 165 was first
occupied in 1812 by Merrit & Corlies, flour merchants.

In 1835 it was the headquarters of Mackie, Oakley & Jennison,
commission merchants who were building the present 181 Front
Street (also numbered 163 and 159 John). The firm altered this
building in the process, extending the granite colonnade along its
shopfront, revising its window pattern to match that of its neighbor and facing its upper stories in new hard brick.

In 1839 Edward G. Faile, a grocer, bought the building together with the Front Street corner, and may have raised the entire group from four to five stories in 1840.

Look today at doors which may belong to the 1835 renovation at the center bay, hung on tapering iron hinges from the
granite piers. (Best seen inside the building.)

Turn right into Front Street, walking north.

The buildings on the west (left) side of Front Street in this
block are to be demolished for an office tower, but those on the
east will be developed, together with Schermerhorn Row and the
other structures in the block, by New York State as part of the
planned Maritime Museum.

186 Front Street

Today the Square Rigger Bar, 186 Front Street, occupies a
building dating from 1807 which was Stephen Allen's sail loft and
store. Allen was born in New York in 1767 and apprenticed as a
sailmaker at age twelve, and had a good talent. He prospered during the War of 1812 providing sail cloth for the United States
Navy, and after the peace he became active in City government.
He was New York's mayor between 1821 and 1824.

The ground floor of this Front Street store was altered in the
Greek Revival manner after Allen left it, and now the shop front
is stucco covered.

189 & 181 Front Street

Across the street, the buildings at 189 & 181 Front Street
were built as a pair in 1835-36. The corner building has a sixth-
floor "classical attic" added in 1917, together with a new ground

View of Brooklyn, Long Island, 1847. From atop the U. S. Hotel, the artist's vision arches over the South Street neighborhood (Schermerhorn Row in center foreground), takes the river at a sweep and settles minutely on the newly urban Brooklyn waterfront which melts gently to rural landscape in the distance. A horse car pulls up at Fulton Street, a ferry glides from its slip, a Black Ball packet lies at our Pier 16. (The New York Public Library.)

floor infill, but the colonnade along the street formed by the massive granite piers is the Greek Revival original.

At 189, beneath the old wooden loading platform you can see, still in place after years of disuse, the channeled granite trough which caught rain from the downspout, splashing it across the flagstone sidewalks and into the muddy street, paved in those days in cobble and earth. Looking closely you can see a rusted remnant of the cast-iron grating which once covered the areaway. The gratings, though difficult to walk over, let light reach the cellar windows.

Number 189 was built for Josiah Macy, a shipmaster turned merchant in 1828, who had had his shop on Front Street since that year. The Macy firm occupied this building until 1885, then moved next door to 191, where they remained past the turn of the century.

193 & 191 Front Street

According to the records, the buildings now standing at Numbers 191 & 193 are the same buildings which stood there in 1793, the first year for which there are recorded tax assessments on these lots. When built, they were two stories high with peaked roofs. Both buildings have visible surfaces of the 1870s, and are late Victorian in style with their "Philadelphia" face brick, cast-iron shopfronts, and the imposing metal cornice and cast-iron window lintels at No. 193. The upper story of 193 is unusually high, with enormous windows across the front. Although its iron ornament is contemporary with its cornice and other detail, a view made in the 1840s shows that it already had an attic as tall as the present fifth floor. One of the oversized double-hung windows is thrown wide open in the view, suggesting that the floor then had a special human use and was not relegated, like most top floors, to storage. Between 1804 and 1816, the leading mercantile firm of Minturn & Champlin occupied this pair of stores.

197 & 195 Front Street

These are Schermerhorn Row buildings.

Here you come again into Fulton Street looking north to the empty lot.

Fulton Street and Market, from Megarey's Street Views, 1834. The best early view of Fulton Market and Schermerhorn Row, this one gives a picture of a quiet Fulton Street that is belied by contemporary descriptions of its hustle and noise. (The New York Public Library.)

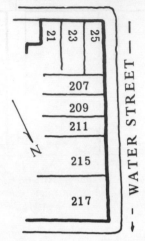

MAP 2

17 & 19 Fulton Street (demolished)

Here is a case where the bulldozer got the best that the block-front had to offer. Demolition proceeds with unerring good taste—time after time a street's proudest buildings are selected and sentenced, often leaving their empty lots painful holes in the street wall. A pair of exceptionally handsome Federal style buildings with arched doorways and balustraded hipped roof formerly occupied these lots.

21, 23 & 25 Fulton Street

These stores are late examples of the Greek Revival commercial style dating from 1845-46. Like the earlier ones, the ground floors here are *trabeated granite* (post and lintel construction), but look closely at the capitals and see, instead of a moulding, a plain concave profile that is plainer than many of the earlier ones and somewhat Egyptian in feeling. The sextant sign aloft at the corner of 25 heralds the Museum Book & Chart Store, echoing the sign used by Edmund March Blunt, nautical bookseller whose shop

MAP 2   21

"Trabeated" construction is synonymous with post-and-lintel. The typical shop of the Greek Revival period was composed of vertical granite piers carrying a horizontal granite lintel. (Drawn by Roger Campbell.)

"at the sign of the quadrant" stood diagonally across the Fulton-Water Street intersection early in the 19th century.

Look up Fulton Street to the white and glass skyscraper on the southwest corner of Water. In 1833, Stephen Holt opened one of New York's grand hotels on this site, its gleaming marble walls and immense size making it "a wonder of New York" according to a contemporary paper. From its cupola flashed the semaphore signals of one of the City's early "telegraph" stations, and it utilized an early system of elevators between its floors. Marvelous as this "public palace" was, it was heavily mortgaged and failed, but was reopened in 1839 as the United States Hotel. It stood until 1902 when it was demolished for the building that preceded the Cocoa Exchange on the site.

Turn right, walking north into Water Street.

Try to slice through history to 1720, when the land on your left, between Pearl and Water Streets, was the eastern limit of Manhattan Island. You are standing where the docks of the Cannons, the Livingstons and the Ellisons broke into the River behind their Pearl Street buildings. That year, though, these landholders were to erect "a good wharf or street of thirty feet" which was shown completed on the Bradford map of 1731. Water Street was finally widened to its present width and paved with cobblestones as far north as Peck Slip, two blocks from here, in 1788-89.

*Nautical book and chart
shop of Edmund March Blunt
at 202 Water Street, corner
of Fulton, circa 1815.*

Holt's Hotel, view from Mechanics Magazine, *January, 1833.
One of New York's first great hotels, this one preceded the legendary
Astor House by three years. A steam-powered hoist for lifting baggage
made its towering six-story height practical.*

MAP 2   23

Portable Forges and Bellows—Queen's Patent.

The best Forge in market for Blacksmith's work, Boiler Makers, Mining, Quarrying, Shipping, Plantations, Contractors on Railroads and Public Works, Coppersmiths, Gas Fitters, &c., &c. Also an **Improved Portable Melting Furnace**, for Jewellers, Dentists, Chemists, &c.

These are the only Forges constructed with sliding doors, to protect the fire from wind and rain when used out-doors, and for perfect safety and free escape of smoke when used in-doors. They are compact for shipping. Circulars, with particulars and prices, will be forwarded upon application.

FREDERICK P. FLAGLER,

Manufactory, Peekskill, N. Y.   Sole Manufacturer, 210 WATER STREET, N. Y.

Frederick P. Flagler was one of the many
Water Street stove and boiler dealers of the 1840s.

The block on your right began to be filled by the owners of the water lots granted early in the 1750s, and the shore line pushed farther into the river. Little frame houses and houses with brick fronts were common on this stretch of Water Street during the 18th century—we find them described in property transfers.

In the late 1820s the character and tempo of Water Street in this district began to pick up. Edmund Blunt wrote in the *Picture of New York or Stranger's Guide* (1828) that Water and Front streets were "occupied by wholesale grocers or commission merchants, iron dealers, or as warehouses for the storage of merchandise and produce of every description." Soon, though, the wholesale grocers and commission merchants were crowded out of the Water Street segment between Fulton and Peck Slip, as that stretch became the undisputed emporium of New York's stove trade: in 1840-41 there were 19 stove dealers here, a count which had risen to 29 by 1851! Most dealers supplied various types of stoves, grates and ranges, and offered additional stocks of miscellaneous ironware, tinware, zinc, lead and copper. Some occasionally advertised as plumbers. (Originally this designation applied broadly to anyone who dealt or worked in lead.)

Granite blocks form a basin to flush rainwater from down-spout to street at 211 Water Street. (Tom Nyulasi.)

★**Numbers 207, 209 & 211 Water Street**

This range of Greek Revival stores is among the best of the type remaining in New York, and it is certainly among the best preserved. In detail the stores are quite similar to Nos. 181 and 189 Front Street, built in the same year. This row was built to-gether for different owners in 1835-36, the vintage year for this City's Greek Revival warehouses.

The granite steps, piers and lintels of the ground floor are well-proportioned and handsomely tooled. The scoop-troughed rain basins that were a practical part of the original arrangement have been restored to their correct positions. Number 211 has the

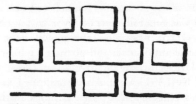

Brickwork laid in Flemish bond. This bond is common on New York buildings prior to 1830, though in this neighborhood a number of later buildings use it. It is distinguished by alternating "headers" (the short face of the brick) and "stretchers" (the long face) within each course. (Drawn by Roger Campbell.)

MAP 2   25

Ithiel Town's 1829 design for the silk store of Lewis and Arthur Tappan on Pearl Street, drawn by his partner A. J. Davis. This store set the style for standard commercial architecture in New York.

original slip sill under the large shop window on the left side. Also of granite is the exceptionally good classical *cornice* (uppermost crowning feature) shared by the three buildings.

The brick used in the row's upper stories is harder and firmer than that of Schermerhorn Row, but not so hard as the pressed brick used to reface the adjoining 21-25 Fulton Street buildings. It is laid up in *Flemish bond* (the outer face alternates the long side of a brick with the short end in each course), a bricklaying technique which was generally out of favor with architects by the 1830s. After Ithiel Town designed the granite store at 122 Pearl Street for silk merchants Lewis and Arthur Tappan in 1829, this trabeated ground floor arrangement became the standard design prescribed for all New York commercial buildings, and any mason could build such a store by studying examples on the streets and in the builders' handbooks. This row is probably the work of such a mason, possibly David Louderback, who bought the property at 211 in 1835 and held it in his estate until 1883. Number 207 is the Museum Model Shop. Bowne & Co., printer and stationer, an operating shop and printing office based on its 19th century prototype, is at No. 211.

213-215 Water Street

Next to the row, this heraldic Italianate building, full of the umbrageous vigor of the cast iron period, proudly asserts its 1868 construction date high in the pediment above its fifth floor. On the street of stove dealers, and built as the warehouse for a tin and metal company, its deeply modeled facade is of carved limestone above the ground floor, cut to resemble iron!

The yellow brick building on the corner, built in 1914, stretches the full depth of the block, covering the original Livingston water lot grant of 1750.

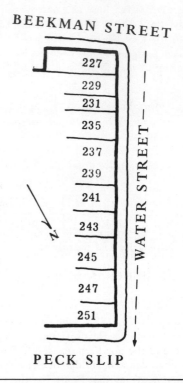

BEEKMAN STREET

227

229

231

235

237

239

241

243

245

247

251

WATER STREET

PECK SLIP

MAP 3

MAP 3   27

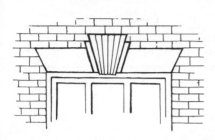

A splayed window lintel with reeded double keystone. Supporting the wall above a window opening, a lintel is an important architectural element, often treated decoratively. Because of its outslanted sides, this type of lintel is "splayed." At the center is its keystone, lined in a "reeded" pattern. (Drawn by Roger Campbell.)

Continue north on Water Street, passing Beekman.

Beekman Street existed here as a narrow dock and alley called the Crane Wharf until 1824, when the street that ended at Pearl was extended to the East River, absorbing the old alleyway. When the wharf became a street, it was widened by removing the buildings which stood until then along its north side.

227 Water Street
A modern brick ground floor on this building at the northeast corner of Beekman and Water completely disregards its age and scale. Its first occupant, here in 1798, was sailmaker Augustus Wright.

229 Water Street
Next door is a ship chandlery built in 1801. Though the upper stories have been covered with sand paint, you can still see the fine late-Georgian, early-Federal period splayed window lintels with reeded double keystones. The ground floor has the plain granite piers of a Greek Revival shopfront.

★SCHERMERHORN SHIP CHANDLERY
243 Water Street
The water lot of William Beekman was divided and passed out of that family on July 20, 1795, when the southern portion was sold to Ebenezer Stevens, a Revolutionary general who became a liquor merchant; and the northern portion to Peter Schermerhorn the elder, ship chandler and builder of Schermerhorn Row. The 1795 conveyance mentions that "part [of the property] is made land, and the soil under the water to be made ..." By 1797 the block had been completely filled, and by 1800 Peter Schermer-

horn was occupying his new store at 243 Water Street. Apparently the building was not a "store and residence," as was fairly common here in the late 18th century, because Schermerhorn, who was well-to-do, was by then living on Broadway.

The Schermerhorn chandlery stayed at 243 until some time after the death of Peter the elder in 1826.

The brownstone-quoined passage entrance with its double keystoned lintel between Nos. 241 and 243 indicates that they were originally built as a pair, and the history of the land suggests that a similar pair may have stood at Nos. 237 & 239. Until 1941, 241 was four stories tall, but its upper two stories and entire front wall were taken down that year. The passage led originally to a spacious courtyard at the center of the block which may have contained stables and other outbuildings.

Above the ground floor at No. 243 remain the fine original splayed brownstone lintels with double keystones, the tooling on their masonry still visible. The original peak roof was replaced by the existing flat one in 1912 when a Schermerhorn descendant wanted to create a more desirable warehouse.

The exceptionally good detail here, and the unusually hard brick (for New York in 1799) used in the walls indicate that these buildings, when they were unaltered, were among the handsomest along the street.

Behind the bricked-up opening a narrow passageway still leads back from the street toward the center of the block. At the sides of this opening are brownstone blocks set to resemble quoining.
(Tom Nyulasi.)

MAP 3   29

FIG 19

Haughty faces cast in terra cotta gaze down from the fourth floor at 251 Water Street, where they form the keystones centering the arched window openings. (Susan Stephenson.)

245 Water Street

This warehouse was built in 1836 after an older building on the site had been ruined by fire. Although its upper stories were rebuilt, and the massively bracketed metal cornice added, it still has the ubiquitous granite ground floor of the 1830s.

245 Water was built for the important copper firm of Hendricks & Brothers, sons of Harmon Hendricks, who had provided the copper sheathing for the *Savannah*, first trans-Atlantic steamship, and for several of Robert Fulton's steamboats. By the 1830s, when Uriah Hendricks and his brothers took over the firm, their business had shifted from the naval trade to the locomotive industry, which was supplied with copper boilers and other parts by the Hendricks firm.

247-249 Water Street

A coppersmith was also housed in this building, which presents a less altered aspect of the Greek Revival type. Note the cornice above its ground-floor lintel with its unusually rich moulding. At the center bay there remains the granite slip sill and possibly the original double-hung shop window.

251 Water Street

On the southeast corner of Water Street at Peck Slip, stands one of the handsomest buildings in the district, built in 1888 by architect Carl F. Eisenach. It was designed for a ground-floor store with apartments for eight families above. Distinguishing the stairway entrance on Water Street is an elaborately cast foliate terra cotta tympanum announcing the street number. The double doors with their massive hinges are probably original. Broad Romanesque Revival arches battered out where the walls meet the ground, with moulded bricks and chamfered corners, opened into the ground-floor store on Water Street and Peck Slip. Terra cotta lintels above the fourth-floor windows are enlivened by keystones whose haughty faces monitor the business of the street.

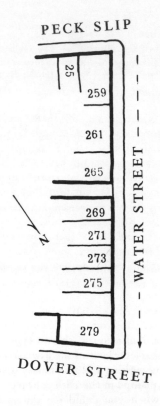

MAP 4

MAP 4   31

Cross Peck Slip, "one of the principal wharfs in the City" in 1789, on Water Street.

In this intersection the City's first brick market was built in 1763 for the convenience of wealthy William Walton and his neighbors on Pearl Street.

261 & 263 Water Street
Built in 1847, these were among the last warehouses built in the then passé Greek Revival mode, their plain piers and un-moulded stepped ground-floor lintel representing one of its simplest forms.

265 & 267 Water Street
The original Victorian double doors with their detachable night shutters now permanently in place remain at Nos. 265-267 (built in 1872) and the original lock with its rectangular escutcheon plate can still be seen on the northernmost door.

269 Water Street
Where the garage at No. 269 is now, the boathouse for the Walton mansion on Pearl Street stood on 18th century Walton's Wharf. The 19th century warehouse here was the plumbing establishment of Thomas Dusenbery in 1845, well known for the sumptuous bath fixtures he made for houses utilizing the pumped-in water supply that the completion of the Croton Aqueduct brought to New York in 1842.

270 Water Street
Number 270 housed at mid-century the rag warehouse for the famous Cliff Street paper manufacturer Cyrus W. Field.

★ JOSEPH ROSE HOUSE AND SHOP
273 Water Street
Amidst the visual confusion of this street on which buildings of vastly different character jar and shadow each other, one building stands practically reeking with the musty dampness of age, its foundations solidly planted in the 18th century.

Imagine a day when you could see the surface of the East River sparkling through the passages and the empty lots on the right side of Water Street, and the graceful sloops resting at anchor off the wharfs beyond. The little building at No. 273, now so oddly narrow, was here then. Certainly the most ancient structure in this neighborhood, it is one of the oldest on Manhattan Island, and was in the vanguard of the northward-creeping commercial district when it was built around 1773.

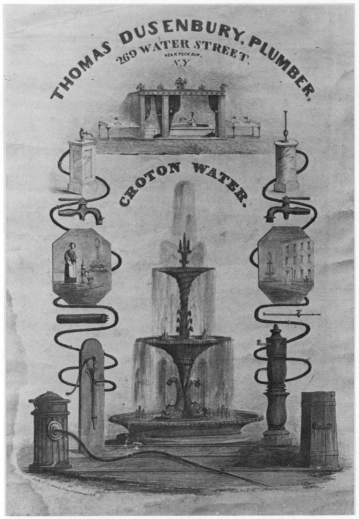

Thomas Dusenbery's sleek plumbing fixtures in the classical mode were sold at 269 Water Street in 1845.

MAP 4   33

In October of 1771 this lot was sold to Joseph Rose, a mariner, who filled land enough to build on and later extended a wharf beyond. By 1773, Rose's advertisements from this address began to appear in New York newspapers.

A 1778 survey by Gerard and Evart Bancker includes a valuable description of the building which stood next door, then connected to No. 273 by a small "arched-over alley." As the two buildings were built together, probably as a pair, the description of its neighbor probably fits No. 273 as well.

The first City Directory, published in 1785, lists Joseph Rose, then a distiller, as the occupant of the building with merchant William Laight next door. In 1789, though Rose's possessions were in the building, it was occupied principally by Abraham Walton, who was the nephew of William Walton, merchant prince of colonial days who had built the palatial Walton House just a block inland from this spot in 1752.

Abraham Walton was a vestryman of Trinity Church and a delegate to the First Provincial Congress in 1775, and at the end of the Revolution had become a merchant. In 1789 he was awaiting the completion of his "house, wharf and store" which was being built two doors south of this building, at the present No. 269. In 1790, Walton had taken up residence in his own new house, leaving this one vacant for some time.

Isaac Rose, son of the builder, ran an apothecary (prepared medicine) shop here from 1796, then in 1807, at the death of the father, the building was sold to lawyer Elisha King, who rented it. In 1812 it had a shoe store on the ground floor with a boarding house above.

The first floor of the building retains the original doorway on the left hand side; and the tiny, oddly shaped window with the broad, blank wall above on the right side suggests the location of the little alley.

Between the first and second floors is the brownstone *stringcourse* (a horizontal band), a characteristically Georgian embellishment and a rare survival. A similar brownstone band above the second floor runs just below the original eave line. The second floor windows retain their original plain splayed brownstone lintels.

A Buildings Department record for 1904 describes the building as having brick walls front and rear with frame sides. At that time it was given added height by raising front and rear walls to the height of the ridge of the old peaked roof.

The Joseph Rose house and shop, the third oldest building on Manhattan Island, still stands at 273 Water Street. It was built three years before the Revolution, in 1773. (Susan Stephenson.)

The ancient building, moss growing in its mortar, dreams in the shade of Water Street, seemingly unconscious of its 20th century additions, oblivious to the architectural cacophony pressing around it. All the history of New York has happened around it— the incredible growth of its neighborhood in the first quarter of the 19th century, the babel of the years of foreign trade and the different babel of the markets, then the fish men, and now the gentle quiet of neglect.

279 Water Street

At the corner of Dover Street, at 279 Water, McCormack's Bar has occupied one of New York's rare wooden buildings for more than half a century. Peter Loring, a grocer, bought this land in 1801, and city directories began to list him resident here that same year. The interior and exterior were radically altered in 1888 when it was converted from a store and hotel into a three-family house. The novelty siding and exterior decorative detail date from that alteration.

Here at Dover Street you stand virtually beneath the massive pylons of the Brooklyn Bridge, designed by John Roebling and built at great cost and amid nearly unprecedented fanfare from 1867-1883. By the 1860s the old Fulton Ferry had reached its capacity, though it ran until 1924, but the demand for passage between Brooklyn and New York was increasing tremendously

Currier and Ives, "The Grand Display of Fireworks . . . at the opening of the Great Suspension Bridge between New York and Brooklyn . . . May 24th, 1883." Like sunbursts and illuminated jellyfish in the night sky over the Brooklyn Bridge, the exuberant pyrotechnics of the 19th century crowned a red-letter celebration day. (The New York Public Library.)

due to a steady flow of families following the merchant princes to the suburbs, Brooklyn and Queens.

When the bridge was planned and built it became more than just a span of steel and granite linking the opposite banks of a river. It was symbolic of the Victorian urge for connection: the telegraph cable, the transcontinental railroad, the canals; all were the arms of Technology linking the world's far-flung ports, sung by poets. "The earth be spann'd, connected by network," wrote Whitman; and Hart Crane's "To Brooklyn Bridge" saw in the soaring structure the essence of the freedom born of movement.

On the 24th of May, 1883, the City of New York opened the bridge with a holiday celebration, the day crowned by the most extravagant pyrotechnic display ever staged here, supplied by the firm of Detwiller & Street.

Before the first stone was laid for the first bridge tower, Wash-

The baronial Walton House had, by the time this view was drawn by architect A. J. Davis in 1830, become a respectable boarding house. (Museum of the City of New York.)

MAP 4   37

ington Roebling prophesied that it would become a national monument, and so it is. But it belongs most to all New York, and to this neighborhood into which it was born and over which it has loomed for more than 90 years.

★ THE WALTON HOUSE
Formerly 326-328 Pearl Street (demolished)

Just one block inland from this Dover-Water Street intersection, near the place where Cherry, Pearl and Dover meet forming oddly angled blocks, stood a house from which came an early influence on this neighborhood's growth, a house so grand that its fame had spread to England before the Revolution.

Wealthy New York merchant William Walton, whose portrait painted by Thomas Wollaston hangs in the New-York Historical Society, built his house of imported yellow brick with brownstone trim in 1752. His house was decidedly Baroque in character, with the Walton coat of arms carved in stone above the entrance porch. Gardens stretched down to the East River, and across Pearl Street were the mansion's extensive stables and carriage house.

Accounts of lavish entertainments given here by the Waltons confirm the lusty character of 18th century amusements, even in the most elegant of houses. William Livingston wrote of the "ten sunburnt virgins, lately come from Columbus, Newfoundland," who formed one of the chief attractions at an early "wasel frolic."

Powerful William Walton had built his mansion well north of the fashionable district, and by 1763 he and the others who had joined him in elegant isolation felt the inconvenience of having to travel some distance to a public market. Their petition to establish a new one in their own neighborhood at Water Street and Peck Slip where the Long Island farm boats arrived was immediately approved, and the public market house which went up there was the first brick market in New York.

In 1784 the Walton House was the first home of the Bank of New York, and in 1797 when the Bank was moved to Hanover Square, it became a boarding house which slid further from elegance as the years went by.

The stately old mansion, having spent more years as a transients' lodge than as a family seat, was finally demolished in 1881, when it stood in a run-down district of old shops and tenements.

Returning to the route of the Tour, walk east along Dover Street to the corner of Front.

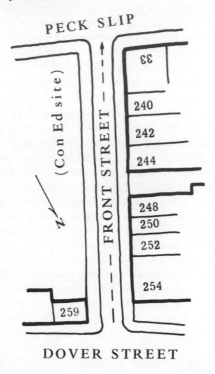

MAP 5

Several buildings have recently been lost from this segment of the walk. Their demolition was a sad loss in this neighborhood where every building has its own distinction, its own particular character.

Turn into Front Street, heading south.

You are standing in the block where the "great conflagration" of December 27, 1853, broke out in the "Novelty Bakery" establishment of Treadwell & Sons at 242 Front, ruining many of the buildings on this street front and on Water and South streets.

MAP 5   39

Even more disastrously the fire burned to the water line the celebrated *Great Republic,* then the graceful queen of the seas, the
largest sailing ship in the world. She had been launched just two
months before from the East Boston shipyard of Donald McKay,
and was bound on her maiden voyage to Liverpool. She had been
docked at the foot of Dover Street since late November taking on
cargo. While on public exhibition at her berth, the *Great Republic*
had netted a considerable income by admitting on board around
40,000 spectators who had come to South Street to see her at the
rate of twelve and a half cents a person.

At about 1:00 a.m. on the freezing cold morning of December
27th the bakery fire was discovered. 242 Front Street couldn't be
saved, and by the time the fire companies arrived, the blaze had
spread next door. Defying the firemen's efforts, the flames had
soon gone through to Water Street, then across to the east side of
Front Street and through the block to South Street. From there
it was only a matter of time and wind before the news in the
"Fourth Dispatch" to the New York *Times* became inevitable:
"The fire is still raging with unabated violence. . . . The mam-
moth clipper, *The Great Republic,* is on fire, and will in all probability be totally destroyed! . ." Still later came the report that
heralded her doom . . . "the masts have fallen and the deck is
burning."

The Great Republic, *fully rigged and ready for her maiden voyage, lies at
anchor in Boston or New York late in 1853.*

Next day, the pyrophile reporter wrote her requiem: "A ship on fire at any time is a grand scene, but the appearance is very remarkable when contrasted with the dark sky of early morning. The falling masts of the *Great Republic* was a sight than which nothing could be more magnificent."

Under more normal circumstances, this section of Front Street was filled with provision shops of various types: pickle dealers, meat packers, grocers, flour merchants and bakers predominated during the mid-century golden age of shipping.

One man had much to do with the proliferation of the flour and bread sellers here. David Lydig, one of the "bold race of merchants that built up New York," went into business at Peck Slip in 1789, living above his store in the early days. Later he owned a fleet of Hudson River sloops in which he brought to his New York wharf the flour ground at his own mills at Buttermilk Falls, near West Point. His immense success as a flour merchant was due to his exploitation of fast Hudson River transportation. Lydig had the foresight to sell his sloops and gradually retire from business as the Erie Canal neared completion, aware that flour far cheaper than he could supply would soon be coming from the farmlands of the western states.

With the flour landing here at Dover Street, bakers could be assured of a good supply, and were encouraged to locate their shops nearby.

259 Front Street

The only building now standing on the east side of Front Street, No. 259 (and 34 Dover Street), stands on the site of David Lydig's flour wharf, and was built for him around 1808. The rest of the Front Street side of the block was demolished for the Consolidated Edison transformer station to be built here in the near future.

242 & 244 Front Street

The west side of the street suffered extensive damages in the 1853 fire and these buildings where the fire broke out were completely burnt and rebuilt. The cast-iron columns on the ground floors of these buildings are typical of the 1850s, and once had bolted-on leafy capitals, now missing. The columns at 242 still carry the applied ornaments within their round-arched vertical panels.

MAP 5   41

Passing the scene of the fire, walk on to Peck Slip, named for Benjamin Peck, whose house and wharf were here early in the 18th century.

Long Island produce boats had docked at Peck Slip long before the establishment of the 1763 market, and the site was an important landing for Long Island river traffic through the steamboat era.

Until 1817, Peck Slip was open to Water Street, and the buildings then standing on either side looked out over the masts of unloading schooners and brigs.

Peck Slip near South Street, pictured in D. T. Valentine's Manual for 1857. The four-story building at the corner of South Street, Number 151, now stands by itself, its neighbors demolished in 1962.

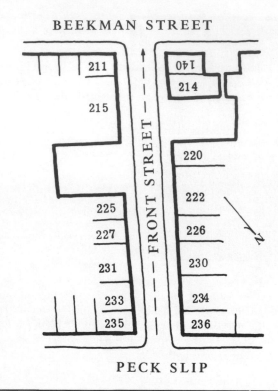

BEEKMAN STREET

FRONT STREET

211
215
225
227
231
233
235

140
214
220
222
226
230
234
236

N

PECK SLIP

MAP 6

Walk on along Front Street past Peck Slip.

235 Front Street

The building on the southeast corner of Front Street and Peck Slip, built in 1828-29 for a firm of flour merchants, retains the original Federal type keystoned arch that held its Peck Slip door. The rest of its ground-floor facade was remodeled and the peaked roof raised to a flat five-story height in 1892 by the fashionable architectural firm of Neville & Bagge, who probably added the pressed-metal window lintels at the same time.

232 & 234 Front Street

Numbers 232 & 234 Front Street, a double building on the west side, was built under a single street number in 1816. That

MAP 6   43

*Once the graceful Peck Slip
entrance to 235 Front Street,
this arched door is no longer
needed, and presents an
unwelcoming cement wall
to today's walker.*
(Tom Nyulasi.)

year it was assessed to Gershom Smith, a grocer who had occupied an earlier building on the same site as a tavernkeeper. In 1891, when the front of the building was repaired to correct bulging walls, the building was occupied as a stable, with carriages on the ground floor, horses conveyed aloft by hoist to the second floor, and fodder stored in the loft.

226, 224, 222 & 220 Front Street

These buildings on the west side of Front Street, and together with the garage replacing Nos. 223 & 221 on the east side, are part of the extension of the water lot purchased from William Beekman in 1795 by Ebenezer Stevens and Peter Schermerhorn. In 1797 the wharfs were on the east side of Front Street, and in 1798, Schermerhorn and Stevens built their Water Street (237-243) and west side Front Street (220-226) buildings. In 1800 Schermerhorn's business was in 243 Water Street and Stevens' in 1799 was at 222 Front Street. They had been neighbors throughout most of their business careers, both men were in maritime occupations (Schermerhorn as a shipchandler and merchant, Stevens as a fleet owner and liquor importer) and finally their two families were joined when John Peter Schermerhorn married Rebecca Stevens. Ebenezer Stevens had been a General in the Revolution, and he was elected to the New York State Assembly in 1802. His fleet of ships, which regularly plied the route

MAP 6   44

between New York and the West Indies, included Christian Bergh's *Gypsy* and the brigantine *Prudence.*

216 & 218 Front Street (demolished)

On the side walls of Nos. 214 & 220, flanking the vacant lot, can be seen the shadows of the steep pitched roofs of the pair of buildings that stood until 1962 at 216 & 218 Front Street. Architecturally superior to their much-altered neighbors, these superb examples of early 19th century commercial architecture could have been the focal point in this Front Street block.

212 Front Street

Carmine's Bar, on the corner at 212 Front, was built in 1824, the year Beekman Street was created here. This property became a corner lot, and the structure, then three and a half stories tall, was built with facades on Front and Beekman streets. The original arched door and window openings in the ground floor on Beekman had brick surrounds with brownstone keystones. These arched openings are reflected in the present stucco-covered arcade at ground-floor level—the arches themselves may exist on the Beekman Street side beneath the covering. The building was raised to four stories in 1890, and the old brownstone window sills and lintels were replaced then with the present bluestone.

229-231 Front Street

The large warehouse at Nos. 229 & 231, built in 1838-39, has a fine Greek Revival granite shopfront with heavy moulded cornice on the lintel, and capitals crowning the pillars. The bright hard salmon-colored brick, though its bond is Flemish, appears to be a replacement of the original surface brick.

227 & 225 Front Street

The buildings on the east side of Front Street, 225 & 227, were built for Peter Schermerhorn in 1822, and those replaced by the garage at Nos. 223 & 221 were probably built for Stevens in the same year.

211 Front Street (142 Beekman Street)

The corner building at 211 Front Street (usually designated 142 Beekman Street) is one of the neighborhood's best. With its cockleshell cornice and starfish tie-rod ends, and its keystones sporting fantastic wriggling fish, the building is jubilantly sym-

MAP 6

45

A masterpiece in terra cotta, this vigorously modeled creature symbolizes the Fulton Fish Market above the windows of 142 Beekman Street. (Tom Nyulasi.)

bolic of the Fulton Fish Market, which was enjoying a high moment in its history when this structure was built for a Schermerhorn descendant in 1885.

George B. Post, who studied architecture in Richard Morris Hunt's office and was later famous for his New York *Times* Building (1889) and New York Stock Exchange (1904), designed this building and its Beekman Street neighbors at Nos. 146 & 148. Its first occupant was fish dealer Samuel T. Skidmore, and it has always housed businesses related to the Market. Fish Market men remember when it housed the Western Union office for the neighborhood, essential to the community before the telephone was common, flashing orders and replies back and forth between the dealers and their customers.

If you're here early in the day, you might be lucky enough to glimpse Sonny Ferris, a cooper, at work in his Beekman Street shop repairing the wooden crates he supplies to the local fish trade.

Look down Beekman Street toward the river.

Today's Fulton Fish Market, standing on piles driven in the river's muddy bed, built in 1907 replaces and nearly duplicates the wooden structure of 1868. The Fulton fishermen and merchants were first established on this East River site in 1835, when

MAP 7

the City erected for them a wooden shed so they could receive deliveries and make their sales from the same location. It was the most practical location possible until this century, when the old smacks began to be obsolete and the waters of the East River began to poison the fish which had formerly been kept live in the floating fish cars behind the market.

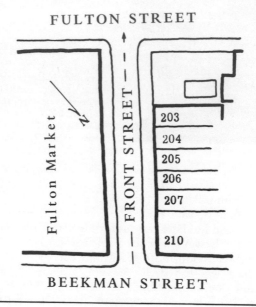

FULTON STREET

FRONT STREET

Fulton Market

203
204
205
206
207
210

BEEKMAN STREET

MAP 7

Continuing south on Front Street, you pass on the east the rear of the Fulton Market block.

It was here on the east side of Front Street that a fire broke out in Sarah Smith's tavern and sailors' boarding house about three o'clock on the morning of January 24th, 1821, reportedly destroying between 30 and 40 buildings, most of them rough wooden houses. Only 12 days before, the City had condemned the block preparatory to the building there of the planned Fulton Market. The fire burned everything on this side of the block "to a heap of ruins," and endangered the vessels moored at the wharfs.

MAP 7   47

*The fourth Fulton Fish Market at its opening in March, 1907,
is pictured in the trade magazine* Fishing Gazette.

All ships, including the sloop of war *Hornet,* were saved by being
pulled out into the river beyond the reach of the flames. After
this fire, pressure was heavy on the Common Council to begin
building, and by 1822 Fulton Market was open. On this side of
Front Street was its rear wing, a handsome one-story arcade with
a two-story peaked roof pavilion crowned above the center by a
belled cupola.

The west side of the street had permanent brick houses and
stores long before the east side was rid of its wooden shanties.
Water lots were granted in the 1750s, Front Street was pushed
through in 1797, and that same year the brick houses began to go
up on the west side of the street, pushing the wharfs out further
into the river.

★207 Front Street

Number 207 is the oldest building on the block, occupied for
the first time in 1797 by Benjamin Stratton Jr., a grocer and
cooper. It is probable that the building was a shop and residence
during the Stratton years from 1797 to 1806. Between 1803 and
1806, Benjamin Stratton Sr., also a cooper, ran a boarding house
here, while the cooperage had moved elsewhere.

Later the building housed Abiel Swift's grocery, then was improved as Jonathan and Joseph Coddington prepared to move in
in 1816.

The first two fish market buildings were wooden sheds on the East River bulkhead. Here is the second of them on a summer afternoon in the 1860s. The fish men pose handsomely for their picture, some dressed in the remnants of Civil War uniforms, while a ferry boat glides to its slip at Fulton Street.

MAP 7   49

Forgotten for nearly a hundred years in the loft of 207 Front Street, this enormous wheel once operated the hoisting mechanism essential to upper-floor storage in these water-front warehouses. Other peaked-roof buildings here have managed to retain these ancient mechanical things to the delight of today's searcher. (John Wisdom.)

Originally two and a half stories tall (the old roofline can be clearly seen on the building's inner walls), it may have been raised before the Coddingtons occupied it, as the details of its roof framing seem to date from the early 19th century. In the attic remains the great wooden wheel, about ten feet in diameter, that operated the hand-powered hoisting system. The wheel still turns, its movements making a weird creaking noise in the dark and dusty silence of the long-disused loft.

In buildings like this one, according to Scoville's *Old Merchants of New York* (1862), the family sitting or dining room was located at the rear of the ground floor, behind the shop. On the second floor was the drawing room and major bedroom, with children's and servants' rooms above.

Boarding houses were commonly kept above stores in this district "for the exclusive convenience of the country merchants" who came to town to order stock in the spring and fall. He adds that the New York merchants often pursued these valued customers by parceling their own salesmen out to board at certain likely houses to make contact with them.

206 Front Street

The building next door was associated with the Howell family for more than a century. In 1795 Matthew Howell was a grocer near this location, on Moore's Wharf before Front Street was opened here. He first occupied this building, which was built as his store, in 1798 or 1799. In 1814, Howell changed his business from a grocery to a military store, and as dealers in guns and gunpowder the Howells were prominent in the community throughout the 19th century. They were apparently the first New York firm to deal in the gunpowder produced by Eleuthère DuPont's powder mills in Wilmington, Delaware.

A water color of 1855 shows the Howell store as a fine Federal style building with separate entrances to shop and residence. By 1880 the building had been damaged by fire, and the front wall was then rebuilt, the peaked roof flattened and the present metal cornice added.

205 Front Street

The granite piers of the 1830s at No. 205 belie its earlier construction date—around 1800—for a firm of wholesale grocers.

204 & 203 Front Street

Now at the end of the block, Nos. 203 & 204 represent an extensive remodeling which transformed the two buildings, previously separate structures, into a hotel behind a unified facade. Number 204 dates from 1799, when it was occupied by Thomas Carpenter, a merchant, and 203 was built in 1815-16 for Peter G. Hart, a grocer who had occupied a building on this site as early as 1806. The present ground-floor arrangement, corresponding window placement, continuous Philadelphia brick face, cast-iron cor-

This lithographic view of 206 Front Street, taken in 1855, shows the building with its original ground floor configuration. The six-panel door opened into a stairhall leading to the living quarters of the upper floors. (Museum of the City of New York.)

MAP 7   51

The employees of the Howell gunpowder shop, newly moved from 206 into 205 Front Street, lounge near their wide-open front door in 1883 or 1884. Above the shopsign, like a logo, a giant firecracker points skyward at an acute angle.
(The New York Public Library.)

nice and incised window lintels date from the 1882-83 renovation of the two structures as a hotel by Theobald Engelhardt for William Wainwright. Little is known about the character of the waterfront hotels scattered throughout the district in the 19th century, but this one was probably of the category described by Thomas Butler Gunn in *The Physiology of New York Boarding Houses* (1847) as "peculiarly characteristic of the lower part of New York." "A showy bar-room, furnished with the usual amount of plate glass . . . occupies the front of the lower story. Most of the boarders . . . are laboring men, having employment in the adjacent wholesale stores, about the wharfs, etc. It is, by express rule, a bachelor establishment." The Museum Ship Chandlery can be found on the ground floor of No. 203.

Reaching the corner of Fulton Street, turn again toward the river, walking past the group of shops established in stalls that were formerly part of the Fish Market complex.

The Museum Art Gallery occupies two stalls, and with the
other small shops already installed, it gives an indication of the
new market function beginning to develop on this site that has
always belonged to trade.

Cross South Street and stand opposite the center of Fulton.

You now have the perspective of the Bennet view (1834) of
Fulton Street, Schermerhorn Row and the Market (Figure 9).
Notice, looking at the view, the neatly flagged sidewalks and
crosswalks. The stone was brought from Connecticut quarries and
its cool gray made a good contrast with New York's red brick
buildings. The few shop signs apparent in the view are subdued in
character, although it was during this decade that they began to
be the exuberant, colorful street features they have been ever
since; and the typical light-colored canvas awnings stretched over
wood stanchions created outdoor space for shops in fair weather.
The comparatively contained nature of the human activity in the
view is denied by contemporary accounts of the shouting hawkers
and thronging people who really informed the scene with their
presence.

THE NEW FULTON MARKET

The high Victorian second Fulton Market building here shown in a mythical landscape, was designed in 1882 by Douglas Smyth, official architect for the City's markets. (The New York Public Library.)

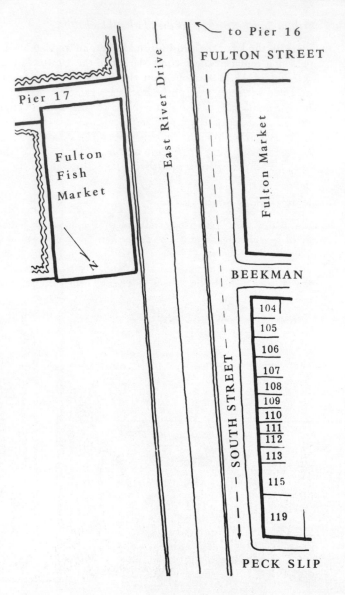

to Pier 16
FULTON STREET
Pier 17
Fulton Fish Market
East River Drive
Fulton Market
N
BEEKMAN
104
105
106
107
108
109
110
111
112
113
115
119
SOUTH STREET
PECK SLIP

MAP 8

MAP 8   55

Walk north in South Street, past the Market block.

You pass on the left the third Fulton Market, an unpretentious structure which replaced the second Market in the 1950s. The E-shaped market of 1822 was open on the South Street side, its courtyard filled with the stalls of the hucksters and "country people." The 1882 market, more compactly built, had a grand High Victorian facade in dark brick and terra cotta on South Street, whereas the present building offers only garage-like doors.

Across the street, the 1907 Fish Market offers one of the City's most breathtaking River views from its east windows.

Continue north along South Street.

Imagine seeing what a British traveller saw here in 1846: "Massive piles of warehouses line the shores; their long and gloomy terraces, upon the one hand confronting the shipping which becomes denser and more dense as we descend. On the other, the broad quays are covered with the produce of every clime; and

South Street at Maiden Lane, from Megarey's Street Views, *1834. This is an early view to suggest the teeming activity of South Street during a working day.*

barrels, sacks, boxes, hampers, bales and hogsheads are piled in
continuous ridges along the streets, which lead at right angles
from the port . . . The scene is now, in point of activity and ani-
mation, beyond all description, whilst the noise is incessant and
deafening; the sailor's busy song, and the drayman's impatient
ejaculation. . . . The vessels which here occupy the slips, are almost all either coasters of the larger class, or engaged in the foreign trade. Passing under their bowsprits, which overhang the
footway, and threaten the walls of the warehouses with invasion,
you pass, one after another, the slips, where lie the different lines
of packets . . . [bound for] the American coastal ports, England,
France, the Baltic, Spain and the Mediterranean, the Coast of
Africa, India, China, South America, the South Seas, Valparaiso
and the Sandwich Islands.''

When has the faraway and unknown ever been so romantic as
on 19th century South Street with its storehouses loaded with
pungent wares and its streets thronged with exotic sailors whose
talk was a pidgin mix of sound?

You see here, past the Market block, between Beekman Street
and Peck Slip, the last complete block of the renowned South
Street stores. Dingy now beneath their rusty metal awnings, a
century and a half ago they were glorious! Banners fluttered from

*This view of South Street, taken in the 1850s, shows the last remaining
block of countinghouses, between Peck Slip and Beekman Street, with
Fulton Market and Schermerhorn Row in the background. At the far right
is 114-115 South Street, the house of Slate, Gardiner & Howell, commission merchants.*

MAP 8   57

their upper stories, ground-floor ware-rooms were in a flux of activity, merchants barked orders at their clerks from platforms at the rear of second-floor counting rooms. (A few of the counting rooms are left; the imperious platforms commanding the forward part of the floor are easily spotted, and certain minor elegancies of trim—a moulded baseboard, a stylishly turned column—set them apart from the storage lofts on other floors.)

104 South Street

Here Frederick Evarts and Rodman Stone had a "salt and grocery store" in 1823, the year the building was completed, and by 1850 when the Age of Sail was peaking the building housed a sailmaker and a ship chandler.

108-113 South Street

This six-building row was built in 1818-19. Like the Front and Water Street buildings directly inland, the southern three were built for Ebenezer Stevens (who used 110 in his business), and the northern three for Peter Schermerhorn. Occupied for the first time in 1819 (111 and 112 in 1820), this row housed merchants, commission merchants and grocers. By mid-century, reflecting the trend through South Street in the shipping community, occupation became denser, and merchants made room for blockmakers, ship chandlers, cotton brokers, sailmakers and "forwarders" to occupy parts of these buildings.

Originally four stories tall with peaked-roof lofts, built of brick in Flemish bond, these buildings all had brownstone-quoined openings for doors along South Street. At No. 108 and again at 112, the brownstone side which defined an original arch can be seen as part of the present yawning garage doors which leave most of the ground floors open holes.

114 & 115 South Street

These two buildings were constructed together and finished in 1840. The stalwart granite piers at either side are original to the building, as is the deep granite lintel above. The pair was constructed by the prominent mercantile firm of Slate, Gardiner & Howell, who occupied 115 from 1840 to 1860, when as Slate & Co., it moved to 114 for its last three years. During the 1880s John J. Flynn ran a bar and lodging house in the two buildings, replacing the original center granite piers with the present store front in 1886.

116-119 South Street

Meyer's Hotel, the handsome corner building on Peck Slip, was built in 1873 for Long Island attorney William H. Onderdonk, by John B. Snook, the English-born architect who had designed and built the original Grand Central Station in 1871-72. Its present name derives from Henry L. Meyer, liquor merchant, who ran the hotel and boarding house in 1881.

Now relatively serene as a hotel and boarding house for men (many of them retired from the Fish Market and related jobs), its early days were not so quiet. Diamond Jim Brady, whose dazzle and flash reflected the boisterous and rowdy side of late Victorian splendor, figures in its bygone reputation; and there are those who say that Annie Oakley's personal celebration of the opening of the Brooklyn Bridge took place on its roof.

Enjoy the flower-basket etched glass panels in the front doors, and look beyond at the magnificently flamboyant dark wood-and-mirrored bar. Here is Victorian style with waterfront character.

Across Peck Slip, another block of buildings, and one with a distinguished history, stood until the summer of 1973, when all but the two corners were knocked down for the forthcoming Con Edison transformer station.

151 South Street

At the corner of South Street and Peck Slip, isolated, stands a little four-story building which was once the hipped-roof termination of a row of three built around 1806-07 for Jasper Ward, a merchant who occupied the inland building (No. 39, now gone) in 1806. Ward had purchased the land on which the buildings stood in 1800, while it was still beneath the water. In 1807, Henry Lambert, merchant, was in business in this corner building. Its soft brick upper stories, laid up in Flemish bond, and its oddly angled hipped roof are original features, while the granite piers at the ground floor replace a brick facade which probably had the typical arched openings. Above the windows, the cap-moulded metal lintels probably replace originals made of brownstone.

The eight buildings which stood between this building at 151 South Street and No. 160 remaining at the Dover Street corner were the first buildings on their sites, dating from 1807 and 1808, though all had been re-faced and their ground floors given the usual granite or cast-iron alterations.

160 South Street.
This was David Lydig's store, built in 1807.

Turn, walking south on South Street.

Begin the walk back toward Schermerhorn Row, and look toward the water as you walk along the shoreline of New York. "There, now, is your insular city of the Manhattoes," wrote Herman Melville, beginning *Moby Dick,* "belted round by wharves as Indian isles by coral reefs—commerce surrounds it with her surf. . . . What do you see? Posted like silent sentinels all around the town, stand thousands upon thousands of mortal men fixed in ocean reveries."

Today the insular city is belted round not only by her wharves, but by the system of highways which girds the lower quarters of the City between the old marginal streets and the river. The F.D.R. Drive has been part of our landscape here at South Street for about 30 years, and unless vehicular traffic in lower Manhattan is curtailed, is likely to remain part of the scene. Through the fretwork of its marching stilts, the water view is framed for us—and to enhance the prospect, the City is presently painting the structure with a color chosen by the Museum.

Walk down Fulton Street, then under the roadway and through the gate to South Street's Piers 15 & 16.

As you come out onto the pier, you'll see the ships ranged along the docks: the ships which are the nucleus of a collection of vessels representing the various phases of the maritime history of this port city.

★WAVERTREE

The handsome iron-hulled *Wavertree* is a traditional full-rigged sailing ship (square-rigged on all three masts) patterned on her wooden ancestors. She's heir to the tradition of deepwatermen built for trade in England and America throughout the 19th century, and at 2200 tons burthen she's just a little smaller than the fabulous *Great Republic* of 1853.

Wavertree was built in England in 1885, one of many metal sailing ships built in Europe well into this century. In America the wood-building tradition was too strong for the introduction of metal construction at the twilight of the square-rigger era. Of the

17,000 square riggers we built in America, only 13 were of iron or steel, and of these only one, the tall bark *Kaiulani*, survives.

Beauty though she is, *Wavertree* is a workhorse of a ship. her voyages often carrying Chilean nitrate for fertilizers. She was dismasted off Cape Horn in 1910, overworked and undermaintained, beat up by her taxing runs, and towed to the backwater of Punta Arenas. There she lived a soft and lazy half-life for about 50 years anchored near to a slaughterhouse, floating in a veritable sea of lanolin which coated and protected her hull. She was a kind of floating warehouse, and her cabin concealed a clandestine gambling center. Years ago, speaking of the *Wavertree* in a pub in Buenos Aires, an old square-rig skipper, Captain Thomas Thomas, reflected on her meaning and her life. "She was an ocean wanderer," he began. "I mean, she had to go everywhere to get her cargoes, she had to do almost everything."

It was in 1967 that *Wavertree* became a symbol for the new South Street Seaport Museum—in June, at the first meeting of the Board of Trustees, the decision was made to try to buy her, to bring her back to life at South Street. Finally in 1970, after three years of strivings and plannings she came. The Museum's newsletter, the *Reporter,* in a glorious special headline, announced that the "impossible" had happened—"The *Wavertree* is here!"

MOSHULU

Next to the workaday thing *Wavertree,* the trim, sleek *Moshulu* looks just what she is—"The ultimate sailing ship"—the winner of the last grain race from Australia to England in 1939. She's a four-masted steel bark, launched in Scotland for German owners in 1904, to carry bulk cargoes from the west coast of the Americas around Cape Horn to Europe. She's big and tough, yet her hull is a fine and delicate thing. She is the finest vessel to come out of the Renaissance of Sail—a limited 20th century reawakening of the love of sheer beauty, power and speed in sailing ships, the last time ship builders really tried to make sail work for modern transport.

Moshulu arrived at South Street in 1972.

LETTIE G. HOWARD

The graceful little fishing schooner appropriately moored near the old Fulton Fish Market is the oldest clipper-bowed fisherman left in America. When she was built (in 1893 in Essex, Mass.) she had as fast a hull as man could build in her time.

Too small to carry the engines of her day, she is pure sailing ship. The *Howard* is partly restored now from her last working years as a motor dragger.

AMBROSE
Ambrose in her working years marked the Ambrose Channel into New York harbor, an entrance made unpredictable and difficult by actively shifting sand bars. She served as the Coast Guard's first Ambrose Channel lightship from 1908-36, a welcoming sight for sailors finally nearing the great port, and then took new position on the *Scotland* station off Sandy Hook.

Ambrose came to South Street in 1968, four years after her replacement by a more efficient albeit less beautiful Coast Guard buoy, and was the Museum's first ship.

AQUA
This sturdy little service vessel, built at Staten Island in 1912, worked originally as a "lighter," unloading deep-draft, hard-to-dock cargo vessels at anchor and carrying freight from point to point within the harbor. She later became a waterboat replenishing fresh-water supplies for the large ships at anchor in the stream.

MARINE SHIP CHANDLERY
Near the pier apron, spanning Piers 15 and 16, is the *Marine Ship Chandlery*, an early concrete barge built in 1919 for the U. S. Navy. The barge was used as a floating repair shop in the Pacific during World War II, and now serves the South Street fleet in the same capacity, under the ownership of Captain William Lacy.

MAJOR GENERAL WILLIAM H. HART
On the far side of Pier 15, the former ferry boat *Hart* serves as classrooms and workshops for the Pioneer Marine Technical School. She was built in 1925 as the *John Lynch* and served on most of the established routes, including the Governor's Island run, until 1970. A ferry boat here at Fulton Street is especially appropriate; the historic Fulton Ferry began here in 1814 and made its last regular run in 1924.

MATHILDA
Little *Mathilda* is a Canadian steam tug, built in 1899 and in constant use until 1969. Though originally used on the St. Law-

rence River, she is typical of the small tugs used in East Coast harbors during the first half of this century.

PIONEER

Pioneer is an iron-hulled coasting schooner built in 1885 to carry iron and steel from a rolling mill to a shipyard on the Delaware River. She was completely rebuilt in the late 1960s and given to South Street in 1970. She now works as a sail-training vessel carrying City youths on two-week cruises as part of their training in the Pioneer Marine Technical School.

OTHER SHIPS

Robert Fulton (north side of Pier 16), the former St. John's Guild hospital barge, newly come, as a gathering place, and soon to be a floating restaurant; her successor, the Guild's new vessel, newly arrived at the City's berth on the south side of Pier 15; *Charles Cooper,* last of the American wooden packet ships, now lying a hulk in the Falklands, owned by the Museum and awaiting funds for her return to New York; *Alexander Hamilton,* now lying at the Brooklyn Navy Yard, the last of the paddle-wheel Hudson River steamers; and *Kaiulani,* American three-masted bark of 1899 owned by the National Maritime Historical Society, may come to South Street in time for Bicentennial celebrations in 1976.

PIERS 16 & 17

The heavy-timbered piers themselves are much a part of South Street: extended and rebuilt at the turn of the century, they too are New York's inheritance from the afternoon of sail. For one period, throughout much of the 20th century, the piers were covered with shed shelters for cargo, rickety in their last years. Now the piers are cleared and once again bright and inviting, open as before to sun and rain, beguiling the reveries of the river watchers.